No Hood Required

A Commentary on Race Relations in America

BRADLEY LONG

Illustrations by Brelyn Giffin

PAGE PUBLISHING, INC.
New York, NY

First originally published by Page Publishing, Inc. 2018

ISBN 978-1-64350-536-7 (Paperback)
ISBN 978-1-64350-537-4 (Digital)

Printed in the United States of America

For Mom and Dad.

My parents were born richly poor. They were rich in love, pride, smarts, and family values but devoid of the opportunities afforded their white counterparts. They worked with what they had. My father was not allowed to finish high school because his parents died by age fifteen and he had to go to work. My mother finished high school and attended college for a few months before family obligations necessitated her leaving college.

They met and fell in love and married. They made a family. They raised a family through sometimes insurmountable odds. They worked hard and were examples to be proud of and to emulate.

This offering is dedicated to them and the men and women who fought the good fight and the bad fight. The heroes and sheroes who stood tall in the face of almost unbelievable struggle to provide a better, more meaningful quality of life for all people on this planet.

They are to be commended and never forgotten. They are men and women of all colors and creeds, from all walks of life, all religions and beliefs, all brave and unselfish.

To their memory is dedicated this commentary on life and race relations in America.

Contents

Introduction

This is my *Strange Fruit*. This is my *American Skin*. This is my *Get Out*.

I was born in the fifties. I was a child of the sixties. I came of age in the seventies. I matured in the eighties. My life forever changed in the nineties. I was hopeful in the new millennium. My eyes were truly opened in 2008. With the election of Barack Obama to the presidency, it became evident that very little had changed. The son of a biracial union, a Harvard graduate, law review editor, community organizer, senator from Illinois, husband, father, and all around good man who just happened to be black, had attained the highest office in the land and become the most powerful man on the planet. After the reign of forty-three white men, number forty-four was a black man. And just like that, it was as if civil rights and progress had never happened. We were back to the 1800s. Hate was the order of the day. We've had presidents that were idiots who were treated with more regard than president Obama was afforded. He was subjected to unspeakable disrespect and abuse as he went about the business of making this a better country and thereby a better world for all people. He had his successes and failures. Every decision he made and act he committed was not perfect. No doubt he has come out of the experience better and stronger, an example to all people, majority and minority. This is my effort to shine a light on the absurd. This is how plain folk think, feel, and reason. I profess to be an expert on nothing. But I know what I know. This is my opportunity to show how ridiculous it is to hate on the basis of physical appearance or philosophical differences or whatever. Differences must not only be tolerated, but they must also be celebrated. There was a time when hate and racism required secrecy in order to flourish. Men killed at

night and wore hoods to hide their identities and ugliness. That is no longer a requirement. The kind of hate we deal in now is public and usually celebrated by the same small minds that brought us slavery and peonage and the current slavery system, prison. The Wall Street exec, the policeman, the store owner, the judge and lawyer, the teacher, the nurse, the politician and the current president of the United States have nothing to fear, and there is no hood required. The beauty of the human experience demands variety in all things. Our differences make us interesting and intriguing. They call out to us, surprise us, thrill us, and make us curious. Ad execs have finally gotten the message. Every other commercial has an interracial expression or theme. The wonder of life itself is made richer by our differences. I vote that we embrace it all. That is the one thing we must pass on to our children and demand that they do the same. Recently, we have gone backward and lost ground hard fought for decades ago. We have allowed hate and stupidity to be the new world order. We have to stop it before we destroy ourselves or someone does it for us.
(Abel Mecropel/Bruce Springsteen/Jordan Peele)

An Introduction to the
United States of America

Welcome to America. Let's review the past. Land of the free and home of the brave. You have entered a land where nothing makes sense. There is no equality. There is no justice unless you can buy it. There is no way to level the playing field unless every adult over the age of twenty were to lay down and die. Anyone who remembers or lived through the last century is forever damaged and twisted by all that they lived through. History has been hijacked and repurposed to fit the scenario. This country was founded on life, liberty, and the pursuit of happiness … if you were white. We are all created equal … if you are white. This is the country that murdered one race while holding captive another. Whites took what they wanted and who they wanted. Nothing belonged to anyone except them. They befriended the natives who helped them adapt to the land. For their efforts, the natives were systematically slaughtered. Their land was taken. Laws were created to make them criminals. The natives fought, but they were no match for these powerful whites. At the same time, slavery—the abusive system of kidnapping foreigners and forcing them to work and submit and beg for their lives and their children's lives while pretending to enjoy the company of whites— flourished. Blacks had to be happy and eager to lick the feet of whites 'cause that was all we were good for, to do the bidding of a race of evil and maniacal people who were lazy and greedy.

Now comes the present. Little black boys and little white boys are treated differently. For identical crimes, the white boy will get probation, and the black boy will get hard time in prison. How can this be? Blacks are an unnecessary annoyance. The whites will eventually kill us off, but until they do, we will fight and educate our families and work to make our lives better until we simply can't do it anymore. We have fought the good fight for the most part. In order to extinguish us, they have been extremely creative. After slavery, there was widespread criminalization of all black activity. This lead to peonage and the prison system we still enjoy today. Along the way, there were cleansings, picnics, Jim Crow, mass murders, and finally, welfare, designed to make us dependent and obedient. Now the police can simply kill us as they have over two thousand times in recent years with no fear of prosecution.

Yes, this is the good life. Welcome to America. Land of the free and home of the slave. Now tell me, how could we possibly be the most intelligent species in the universe? If you listen to God, He is cracking up!

Abraham Would Be Ashamed

To borrow a phrase from Abraham Lincoln, when, in the course of human events, we realize that this here is not working, we have got to do something different. What we have in America is not working. What we do here is not working. How we think is not working. Our laws are not working. Our behavior toward one another is not working. Maybe most of all, our laws are not working.

When those who founded this country left the king's rule, they supposedly sought religious freedom for all, justice for all, and the pursuit of happiness for all. The framers of the Constitution were almost all slave owners. With few exceptions, these founding fathers and mothers believed it was their right to own a human person and bend that person to their will by any means. This thinking runs in line with all those historical figures we now find to be cruel and maniacal and ruthless. The founders were no different from the war-mongers and dictators and kings and emperors throughout history. When the few (slave owners) rule the many (slaves) by force, there is only disparity and hardship and unrest, and finally, revolution.

We are moving in the direction of revolution. Hopefully a peaceful one, but who can tell? The time has ended when the racial majority can direct the lives of the minority, ensuring progress for the former and devaluation for the latter.

There is no peace because those who rule do not want peace. As long as the have-nots are distracted by want and lack and need and scraping out a survival, there will be little peace. Anger and frustration are boiling underneath the reality of police killings, unemployment, disrespect, and being played like puppets. We have tired of being moved about like pieces on a game board. We say game over!

No Hood Required

We like to think that the world is a wonderful place full of opportunity and good will. We are supposed to believe that all things are possible with lots of hard work and some good fortune. These beliefs and truths do not apply to all of us equally. If you are born white, the world is open to you; you have an all-access card. For those of us born something other than white in the United States of America, the reality is quite different. In spite of the so-called progress that has been made, non-whites born in this land of opportunity know that the rules don't apply to us. No matter what you have accomplished. No matter how hard you work. Not even if you are president of the United States.

The reality of life in this United States of America is this: minorities and immigrants are not valued or even welcome here. We are a problem that cannot be solved and will not go away. Regardless of our accomplishments, we are as a boil on the butt of the human white race ... something that requires attention but must be thrust from the lives of those who are inconvenienced by our presence. We don't matter because we are inferior and only marginally useful. Every now and then, we produce some worthy contribution, but it is a short-lived and inconsistent phenomenon that they can't count on or trust in until they steal it and rebrand it.

The fact that this land was "discovered" and was already inhabited meant nothing to the war mongering, greedy, lazy, and ignorant rapists who settled on it.

This country was founded on the slaughter of one race and the enslavement of another. A country whose actions upon these races has had far-reaching and never-ending consequences. A country who ranks itself as the greatest country on the planet. A country who values its citizens according to their stock portfolio, bank accounts, and the color of their skin. A country steeped in tradition and rights and wrongs. A country that promises everything and delivers little to the very people who built this land but get no credit. A country of laws and rules and courts, of checks and balances, and the most broken system in the known world. A country that has its proverbial head up its proverbial butt.

There will be no peace in this world until those born with the ability to discern race have passed on. We are burdened with the scars and the memories of how it was and that has forever defined how it will be. Those who wield great power are unable to relinquish it, and that is what must take place to conquer the beast known as racism. Only the truly color-blind are able to bring about true, lasting, and meaningful change. Only those born of and with the inability to even define color can do the job at which we have all failed since the beginning of time.

On these pages are some truths, some exaggerations, some shameful facts, some opinions, and some debatable statements all about life in America from a sometimes humorous and sometimes shattered-by-reality point of view.

This is my truth. It is not meant to be all-inclusive. Black lives are snuffed out and thrown away like so much trash. Their families receive what amounts to a nominal fee for the inconvenience. White lives who have their sensibilities injured or bruised go to court to win astronomical awards for what amounts to triviality by comparison. How can we explain that to our children? Clearly, in this United States of America, only white lives matter. And possibly blue lives.

The whites who came to settle this country so many centuries ago were weak and lazy and stupid and shortsighted for they could not figure out how to conquer and tame and work this wild land without first the help of the true owners of this land who taught them survival and secondly the involuntary help of slaves imported for their particular needs only. With reckless disregard, they set into motion a legacy of damage unlike any this country has known since. They did not know how to function without the king they left behind. What did they think they would find when they got here? History has proven again and again that greed and want and arrogance rule out over common sense and decency every time. The founding fathers and their fathers were no different from all the megalomaniacs who preceded them as well as those whom they spawned.

How do we reconcile these events and the horrible history that followed? What would you do if your great-to-the-nth-power loved ones were stripped of their humanity and treated as less than animals for the use and amusement of a truly inferior people? To this day, there is no true equity, no balance, no leveling of the playing field, no apology, no reparations, no solution. All the beliefs and reverence of this country are embedded in the document called the Constitution. In this document, slaves were described as property and not worthy of representation.

Since the end of the civil war we, black Americans, as we have come to be known, have had to reassert our worthiness and fight in every decade for our God-given rights. Whether it is for employment, education, a living space, voting rights, a decent wage, or the right to just exist, we have had to fight for what white America takes for granted as guaranteed by the constitution. All the marching and preaching and praying and lynchings and hoping have brought us to today. A day where Nazis and KKK and white supremacists are allowed to publicly spew their hate and sick beliefs and to employ terrorist tactics on the streets of Charlottesville, Virginia, causing the loss of lives. No hoods were required. All this while the president of the United States makes a lukewarm statement regarding the affair but does not give a full throated denunciation of the disgraceful display.

The combination of our president, the head of the DOJ, and the white advisers make for an absolutely perfect breeding ground for one of the antichrists to rear its evil head. The nationalists control the executive and judiciary branches of government. Maybe they control the legislative branch too. We must remain ever vigilant because these men intend to get rid of us by any means necessary. By executive order, creating new laws, using existing laws, or any combination therein, we will know the wrath of evil. These men know evil, and they court evil, power, and domination.

A Short and Simple
Lesson in History

In 2015, the publishers known as Mcgraw-Hill released a sanitized version of American history in a world geography book provided to high school students all over the country, which completely debunked the reality of the American slave trade. The book suggested that the slaves were simply workers who had migrated to America.

Let's examine that fact.

If that were true, why was there a civil war?

Why did 620,000 men die from combat, disease, starvation, and accident during this war?

Why do white people reenact the civil war yearly?

Why does the KKK exist and thrive?

Why were the workers lynched, raped, beaten, sold, and generally demoralized?

Why, after the civil war, was nearly all the workers' behavior criminalized so that the new slavery, prison, could be enacted and profited from?

Why did the workers not simply quit their jobs and move on?

Why were the workers forbidden to learn to read and write?

Why did the workers have no rights?

Why was there no equality as there was for other foreign immigrants?

Why could they not own land?

Why were they bought and sold?

Why were their families destroyed?

It is incumbent upon black people to educate all children of all races and everyone else on what it is that comprises our history.

Obviously, we cannot depend on book publishers, unevolved teachers, or the internet to do it for us. Everyone, especially our own people need to know the truth of how we came to be as we are today.

Let's remain ever vigilant and know what is being taught and alleged about our history. It is bad enough on its own without having our children believe we came here voluntarily and allowed ourselves to be enslaved for hundreds of years and now have barely improved our situation here even though this country has elected a black president.

The more things change, the more they stay the same.

American Dream

White American Dream

- Money
- Homes
- Education
- Freedom of speech
- Freedom of religion
- Freedom to protest
- Law and order
- Safety
- Jobs
- Travel
- Police protection
- Privilege
- Fair playing field
- Life, liberty, pursuit of happiness
- All the freedoms, none of the worry

Black American Dream

- Slavery
- Jim Crow
- Criminalization of all things black
- Unemployment
- Poor housing
- Corrupt law enforcement
- Substandard education
- Gang violence

- Government-sanctioned ripping apart of the family structure
- Disease
- Designer drugs
- Ghettos
- Disappearances
- Murder by cop—the new genocide
- Corrupt politicians
- Gerrymandering
- Electoral college
- And so on
- All the worry, none of the freedoms

The white American dream is the black American nightmare. The white American dream has long been a nightmare for minorities. As the authority for what is right and just and good as well as the moral compass of the world, America is the biggest poser of all.

Having It All

America is a grand delusion wrapped in an illusion. We have intoxicated the world into believing that you can come here and have it all. Here's what we have to offer:

- All the racism
- All the police brutality
- All the crime
- All the political mess
- All the inequality
- All the gun violence
- All the mass/spree killings
- All the tolerance for abuse/hurt/pain
- All the sickness and none of the care
- All the illegal acts committed in public and behind doors
- All the craziness they want to keep others from coming here to get

I say, let them have it all they will soon give it all back, with a quickness as soon as they see for themselves that you cannot live or work or love or worship or feel safe or be healthy or raise children or speak your mind or hold onto your money, etc., etc., etc.

The document that guarantees all that was not written with them in mind. It was written for the privileged race. The idea of mass equality came much later from other forward thinkers. It was met with resistance and bloodshed.

So wake up and change the world you now live in if it doesn't suit you. Coming here will only add to your frustration and sense of powerlessness—unless, of course, you are white and thereby privileged.

A Letter to the USA

Dear United States of America,

It never ceases to amaze me just how hypocritical you can be. You who believe that you and only know what is best for the world. Have you really looked at the example you have set? Let's reflect on how you have helped people during your red/white/blue history.

Your forefathers went looking for a land in which they could be free and escape the taxation of their previous nation. They found what they eventually named America. They very soon found out the land was inhabited by natives. So what! They had weapons and a bag full of tricks to use and then set about to destroy these trusting natives who were in their new world. Their love of money, hunger for power, and huge egos brought about the need to destroy one race and enslave another. In case it is not clear, I mean natives and Africans, respectively.

You hold yourself above the Adolfs, Osamas, Idis, Castros, Kahns, and Ayatollahs, but you are just as they were, all cut from the same cloth, a cloth woven of human misery and soaked in the blood of the weak, the trusting, and the blind.

As history ekes out the real facts with each passing decade the truth and horrors of how you treated your own, how do you keep that flag flying so high? It's so much a part of you that you don't even realize it. No people in America have suffered more or continue to suffer more than the black race, with the exception of the native race. We have managed to survive because we know the identity of the true master and where true power resides.

You owe us, and you owe us big-time. Enough is enough. We don't want your money or your property or your sons and daughters.

All we've ever wanted is to be treated as equals and be allowed to succeed or fail on our own without the monkey wrenches you've thrown in our plans for-seemingly-ever.

In the meantime, go on about the business of the world. Pretend that all here is well and that you are minding and protecting us all and doing a good job. But you know that we know the truth. Love to all.

Sincerely,
The Disenfranchised

The Richness of America

America celebrates its greatness every day in many different ways. America is the best. America is first in all things good. America is the arbiter of all things right or wrong worldwide. America is the shining example of all that is desirable.

Now back to reality.

America is a country predicated on keeping the white race happy, safe, and content in their perceived superiority. America is an experiment gone wrong. We refer to the framers in all issues and disagreements about life, liberty, and the pursuit of happiness.

The framers were a group of white men (and no women) who shaped a country to fit its wants and needs. No thought was given to any other considerations except what the framers believed was right for them. These white men gave no thought nor care to the fact that they came to a land that was already occupied by a people. As poorly as black people have been treated, it is incomprehensible to think what white men have done to the original, indigenous people who really own this land.

White men stole the land. They killed the natives. They lied to the natives. They tricked them and used every scheme known to them then invented some others to rape a race of people and to cheat a race of people and to suck the very life out of a race of people. Only when these natives were finally fully submissive were these white men content in the knowledge that they were the dominant people.

These white men were motivated by greed, the desire to own land and gold. They needed to feel they were the better man. What they forgot speaks volumes. They forgot that these people saved their lives when they could not adapt to the new land they came to steal. These natives taught them survival skills, which served to be their eventual undoing. The natives taught them so well that they did not see what was coming, their eventual destruction and a real effort at bringing about their total extinction.

Today, these brave natives continue to fight for their survival and betterment for all. They know what some don't know. That we are all on this one planet together and will have to work together for everyone's eventual survival. And that we must fight the ignorant and greedy folks that have always cared only for themselves.

We have to. Our very lives depend on it.

Fun Facts

Parents can no longer raise their children to believe that the police are our friends and protectors. The police are now judge, jury, and oh-so-capable executioners.

When you need a murder committed call on the police to find a subject who fits the description. We have a rich history for blaming a black man for every imaginable crime. This tactic is so successful that it's only after he's been shot, castrated, or spent decades in prison that we find out that someone has lied often with the help of the men and women of the legal system.

That blue line is more powerful than the black line as black officers have joined their white partners in the killing and mistreatment of blacks.

It seems we have a whole lot of policemen who cannot tell a wallet or phone from a weapon. What kind of training do these people get? Where are their people skills? Does anything matter other than the safety of the officer? Obviously, no, it does not.

Why should the police demand and expect so much respect? They are often the most horrific of cheats and criminals. So are many lawyers and judges.

It's difficult to tell the difference between police in the USA and ISIS. The job the police are doing amounts to genocide and racial cleansing. The difference is the police don't have to hide. They are seldom charged or tried and are even more seldom convicted no matter how blatant the act or how much evidence exists.

As soon as the number of white men and women killed by the police equals the number of black men and women killed by the police for obscure and ridiculous reasons an apology will be issued.

You Owe Me

You owe me for every man and woman that you forced onto a ship to come here.

You owe me for every precious life lost during those voyages.

You owe me for every soul who could never return to the land of their birth.

You owe me for every man, woman, and child who stood on an auction block.

You owe me for every family you ripped apart.

You owe me for every child who was raised without his or her parents.

You owe me for every man, woman, and child who was abused for your pleasure.

You owe me for every lash that was struck out of anger or dominance.

You owe me for every scar that remained after those lashings.

You owe me for every man, woman, and child lynched out of rage or for your pleasure.

You owe me for every act of senseless and unthinkable abuse at your hands.

You owe me for every act of degradation you used to humiliate me.

You owe me for every child I bore as a result of your lust.

You owe me for every tear shed and every mother's plea to keep her children.

You owe me for each of your children raised by me.

You owe me for every piece of cotton and leaf of tobacco picked by my hand.

You owe me for every brick laid and every building constructed with my sweat.

You owe me for declaring me to be less than a worthy human being created by God.

You owe me for the peonage system you created after slavery was finally abolished.
You owe me for the prison system that took up where peonage left off.
You owe me for the laws you created that made me a criminal and sent me to prison.
You owe me for the banishments and racial cleansings of the last two centuries.
You owe me for the adverse possessions of our land and property after the cleansings.
You owe me for the systematic plan you created to weaken and destroy my family.
You owe me for never leveling the playing field and giving me a fair chance.
You owe me for the violence you have financed and for my leaders that you have killed.
You owe me for that devastating creation known as crack designed for my destruction and sponsored by you.

Because you could no longer own me, you immediately became threatened by me so you set about devising an even more evil scenario. You sought to guarantee that I would never know true freedom, which is not only my birthright but has been earned by my blood, sweat and tears.

You owe me for every second of every minute of every hour of every day of every week of every month of every year of every decade of every score of every century that you have stolen from me by the lies you told, the secrets you kept, the murders you committed, the favor you bought, the cover-ups you engineered, all in the name of America.
You owe me an enormous debt for the price of my dignity. You owe me the kind of debt that you can never truly repay. There are far too many crying out from the grave for justice never received in this life. You wouldn't have enough money if you kept all the printers going from now until the end of time as we know it. It is impossible to correct the unreasonable acts of you and your founding fathers. You

continue to seek to find ways to disenfranchise me. You deny me health care and a quality education. You deny me housing outside of the vertical and horizontal projects and ghettos you herd me into so that you can keep watch over me. You disrespect me when you deny me a job that pays a living wage, when you target me out of fear and anger and spite, when you plot to bring pain, when you threaten my rights granted by God, when you perpetually advance the negative stereotypes and lies that cripple the fresh free minds that just might give me a fair chance one day, when you teach hate. You brought us here by force. We are as you have fashioned us to be. You call us lazy and shiftless and violent and stupid. We are the mirror image of our former masters.

You can't deny it or whitewash it. You've paid the others. Now find a way to make it up to me, because at the end of the day, when it's all said and done, you have treated me in an incredible, unspeakable, and unforgivable manner. You owe me. And you know it.

Anonymous Observation

After
Slavery
Peonage
Racial cleansings
Trampled liberties
Shattered dreams
Freedoms denied
Promises broken
Immeasurable loss
Centuries-old wounds
Countless tears
Conditional surrender
Deadly perseverance
Bottomless sacrifice
Exceptional understanding
Incredible strides
Agonizing patience
And
Unparalleled faith
In 2008, change finally came to America
Land of the free, home of the slave

Pathways

From Slavery to Segregation to Integration to What?

Centuries ago, history set in motion the events that would bring about a world full of extremes. The extremely rich and the extremely poor. The included and the excluded. The good and the bad. The right and the wrong. What have we learned?

We have learned that while life is not always fair for the disenfranchised, there is a redeemer.

We have learned that karma exists and payback is a mother.

We have learned that every once in a while, someone gets what they so richly deserve.

We have learned that good wins out over evil—eventually.

We have learned that what our mothers and fathers taught us was right: play fair.

We have learned that patience can be its own reward if you can be patient.

We have learned that there are dark and malevolent forces at work.

We have learned that these forces are aided by those who seek a return to the past.

We have learned that the promises made by some governments are meaningless.

We have learned that they'll tell you anything to get what they want.

We have learned that they will lie, cheat, steal, and kill to get their way.

We have learned the true meaning of genocide and imminent domain.

We have learned that presidential candidates are masters of spin.

We have learned that what we the people want, need, believe, or care about has nothing to do with elections.

We have learned that we don't have nearly enough amendments to the constitution.

We have learned that we must arm ourselves for the never-ending fight ahead for equality and right and justice and enlightenment if we hope to survive.

We have learned that our path has been and will continue to be dangerous and difficult and may be our final path—but it will be worth it in the short and long run for those we will leave behind and to be certain that this struggle will never be forgotten or whitewashed in history.

Rite of Passage

African Americans/blacks have paid the price to belong and officially take their place in American history, regardless of what the privileged in America think. American citizenship is easier for any race other than the black race. Blacks have more than earned a seat at the table, and yet the struggle continues.

Regretfully, this land of milk and honey, that at one time welcomed all with outstretched arms, has never extended this invitation to the descendants of those slaves who traveled to America as captives.

When will the scales balance for blacks? Well, full and equal rights for blacks is a vague dream that is far in the distance. Blacks have supported the American dream since the revolutionary war. The price that we are still paying for this "rite of passage" is much too costly, too painful, too crippling, and too devastating. It is, in essence, beyond the reach of black America.

Therefore, when one considers hope for tomorrow, that is, all blacks have to count on in these United States of America. In desperation, blacks live and thrive on what has become the random acts of kindness, some inkling of fairness, religion-inspired repentant feelings, guilty consciences, forced legislation, and the reality of a lifestyle that will no longer be tolerated or accepted.

The black man continues to be berated in a manner that questions and diminishes his manhood or womanhood and character. Blacks are forced to live a life screaming out in pain manifested into an element that believes it has the right to rob, steal, or kill its own people because society has given those with this mind-set no way "out" or little reason to strive for the privileged utopia. Living in constant pain has yielded a crop determined for self-destruction.

Although there are so many more who do manage to maneuver through this maize and thrive, but they do so only because "the powers to be" have permitted the jaded rite of passage for some blacks. How pathetic and unfair.

If black America writes its own epitaph, the inscription may appear like this:

> Equality-
> Absent with malice
> Malignant and injurious
> Eroded and decaying
> Rejection ongoing
> Impending acceptance
> Character annihilated
> Aggressive denial

Even though there is no phase of life in America that blacks have not contributed to in some way, we remain hidden figures without the keys to the big house. How dare the black man or woman expect more! Never mind that the black race has earned that rite of passage. Denial does not resolve the problem. This injustice continues to fester. The debt has been paid in full with blood, sweat, tears, and countless sacrifices. Nonetheless, the keys to the portal for equality are still out of reach, and the scales of justice wear a brazen blindfold for black America.

"Your tired and your poor have alway
been here, still yearning to be free."

JULY
IV
MDCCLXXVI

Gates of Hell

ALL YE WHO ENTER HERE
"Welcome, we've been waiting for you!!!!!"

"Even the rats knew it was a pipe dream."

"For sale to the highest bidder.
Minorities need not participate."

AUCTION
BLOCK
500
$

DUMB
DUM
GUESS

"Making America Great Again???"

"I give up."

MPLOYMENT

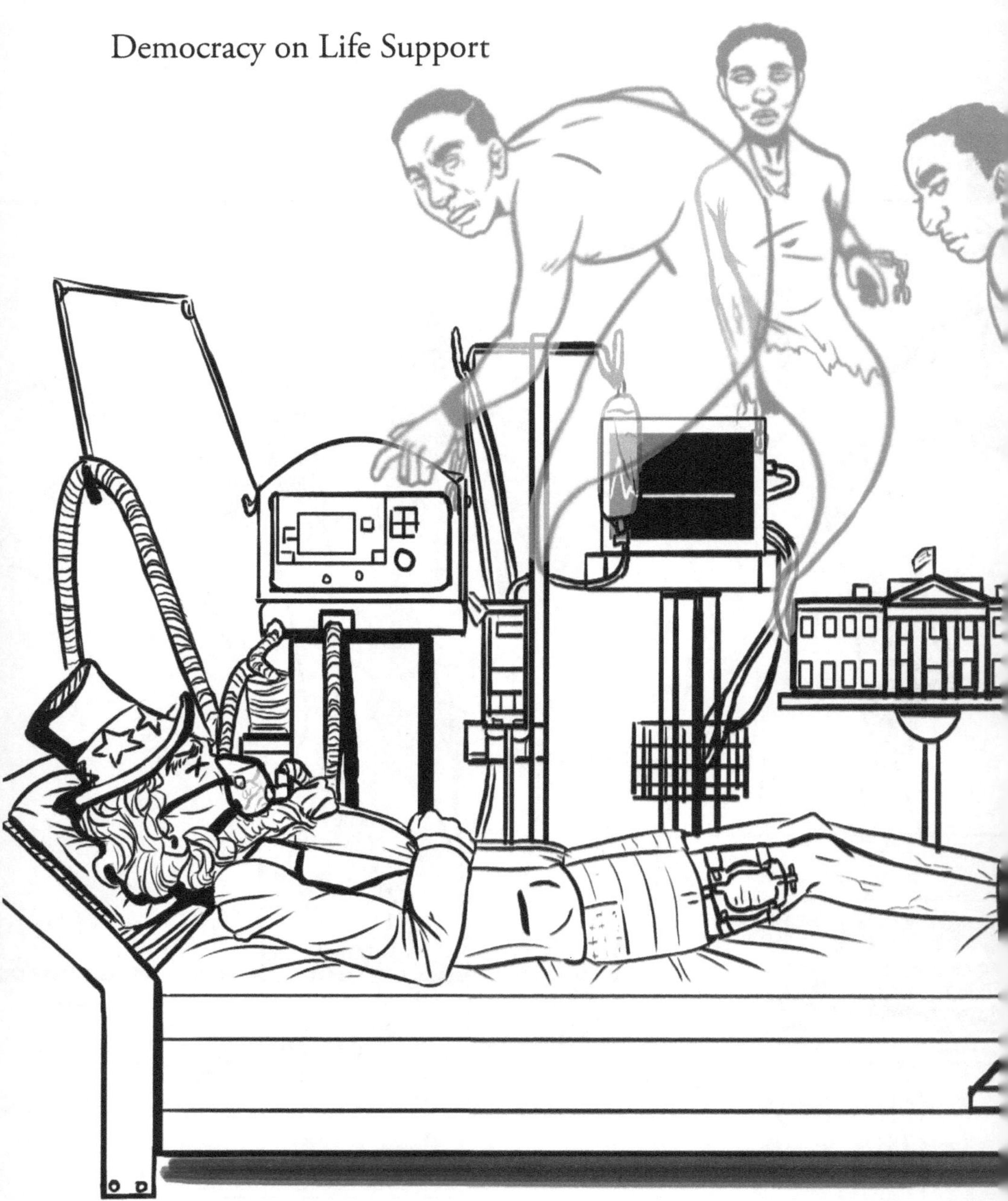

"Rest in peace. You were never ever really alive."

ADECLARATION
UNITEDSTATESOFAMERICA

QUA

Brandon Wilton is a dumb and disgraced news anchor who was fired from a major network for reasons which will become apparent. Now working at a small Southern local station, these are stories he has covered.

Brandon covers: Academy Awards
while Dressed in Blackface

Brandon covers: Barack Obama winning
the Presidency while Dressed as KKK member

Brandon covers: Celebration of Martin
Luther King day while Dressed as Hitler

Brandon covers: Bruce Jenner becomes
Caitlyn Jenner while Dressed as a woman

Brandon covers: Amber alert of missing
child while Dressed as a child molester

Brandon covers: All points bulletin on black man in hoodie sought by police while wearing a hoodie. Brandon is shot and killed while on air by police. They thought his microphone was a gun.

Statue of Liberty

Many people don't know the full history of the Statue of Liberty. The statue is a gift from France to the USA. But the original statue was of a black female with black physical features who stands proudly with broken chains at her feet. This statute was rejected and returned because the white decision-makers believed, and rightly so, that this representation would offend the Southern sensibilities. The statue was returned appearing as we all know it today.

Here's what the Statue of Liberty proclaims:

"Give me your tired, your poor. Your huddled masses yearning to breathe free, the wretched refuse of your teeming shore. Send these homeless tempest-tossed to me, I lift my lamp beside the golden door!"

This is how America has rebranded the Statue of Liberty:

Keep your tired, your poor, your huddled masses yearning to breathe free. Keep the wretched refuse of your teeming shore. Send these homeless, tempest-tossed somewhere else. I lower my lamp and close my gate. The free ride is over.

Reality Check

On November 8, 2016, the USA stepped into the history books by electing the most underqualified person in recent history to the office of the presidency. Underqualified for so many reasons. It was not a proud and calculated move but a critically miscalculated one that is having far-reaching consequences. Given his victory by the electoral college, not the popular vote, this man is set to destroy most, if not all, the advances we have made in this country in race relations on maintaining integrity of the office as well as being the recognized world leader. He is uninformed in the ways of diplomacy. He is used to barking orders have having them followed without question. He is undereducated on the important stuff. He may be the great deal maker in his personal life, but he is terribly unfit to govern. We see this on a daily as he stumbles through his duties and creates more and more controversy and makes less and less sense. He reportedly has a short attention span, does not read for himself, and is addicted to certain television. I believe before it is over, we will learn that at the heart of this mess was the destruction of our democracy by a foreign power. This supposed savvy business man stumbled into this office after getting involved in business and political dealings that he never imagined could come back to bite him and could potentially ruin this country as well as his family and reputation. We are already diminished on the world stage. I don't believe we'll ever recover our former status because every day, he piles on more and more. He has surrounded himself with the kind of unlikely people who have questionable loyalty to country but complete loyalty to a man whose mental faculties are now in question and a small base of voters, some who are not among the best and brightest this country has to offer. The unprofessional manner in which he and others have arranged their white house is pathetic. Where are the safeguards and protocols that would prevent the almost daily embarrassment of this administration? Wanting change is what led to the election of this man. Is this the change that was wanted or needed? I think not. Now it's too late to change. We can't return him to the store because he does not fit. We are stuck with him until he is impeached, or best-case scenario, he grows tired of the scrutiny and quits. Why was he allowed to disregard the norms of campaigning? Why did he not have to release his taxes? Can you imagine if Obama had tried that? This reality show needs to be canceled. The ratings are abysmal. The supporting cast is crude and not fit to serve being out of touch with most of the population. Those closest to him are his worst enemies. They indulge him; they don't make him better. They will bankrupt this country, and we will quite likely not recover. In making America great again, he has wrecked America.

The question begs, when was America ever so great? Was it during slavery? During the slaughter of welcoming natives? The Civil War? Reconstruction? Peonage? The creation of our prison system? Creation of the welfare state? The proliferation of crack? The fight to be educated? The fight to have lunch in a restaurant? Was it when Trayvon Martin was murdered by a jackass? Or when Sandra Blound was murdered by the police? Was it when Eric Gardner was choked to death and got no help as he lay there and died? Was it when we fought in segregated WWII? Was it when Muhammad Ali went to prison for objecting to fighting in Vietnam while our president stayed home and fought those terrible bone spurs in his foot? Was it when we were lynched on the basis of lies or just because someone felt like hanging a nigger? Or was it when our black leaders were attacked and jailed and killed for demanding our God-given rights? Was it when four little girls got blown up in church? Or was it when the president called the NFL players sons of bitches? I could go on, but please remind me, 'cause I forget just when America was so great. And all this time, I thought I was living in a shithole.

Jury Duty

The system is far too broken to allow one man or woman, let alone twelve men and women to sit in judgment of another. The system allows the privileged to have the advantage of good representation that can be bought and paid for. The less advantaged get the law school leftovers who are overworked and underpaid and definitely undermotivated.

Why does a black boy caught with marijuana get fifteen years in prison when a white boy who gets caught with marijuana get probation? How do we justify or simply explain this?

It boils down to racism and who can lawyer the best, who has the best resources to get the judgment they want, who has the most resources at their disposal, who can present the better case in court, who can be the most persuasive, and who is able to bend the law in their favor. It is clear that the average minority citizen doesn't have a chance.

Think about it. How many innocent people are now incarcerated because their lawyer did not have the knowledge, skill, or resources to present a good defense? Now think about this. How many people guilty of horrific crimes and offenses are walking the streets able to reoffend because they could pay for the best defense?

The jury system is flawed. It is not absolute. One can lie to get on a jury and lie to get off a jury. Man should not stand in judgment of man in such a way. We are taught to believe that the American system of jurisprudence is the standard. Far too much injustice takes place under this system to believe this. Law enforcement, lawyers, judges, lab personnel, coroners, etc. Are all humans fallible and subject to error and the pressures of life and poor judgment, all of which factor in the equation of what we call justice.

Let's create a system where jury duty is a paid professional position that requires a course of study with standardized minimums. Remember, the present system was created by the same founding fathers who did not allow white women to vote or serve on juries. Who enslaved an entire race of people for purely economic reasons and who killed an entire race of people just to possess what they owned.

The Lost

Why is it that the world does not stop when a black or brown child goes missing? Why doesn't a national alert go out? Why doesn't the media relentlessly cover the story? Why are rewards not offered? Why aren't the law enforcement agencies and authorities looking for the lost who just happen to be black or brown or anything other than white?

Do we value a little white girl or boy more than a black boy or girl? On what do we base this opinion? Aren't one mother's tears just as painful as another's no matter the color of those tears?

When will we finally learn the true meaning of equality? Will it be just before we lay down to die after a lifetime of hate and hurt? Can we reverse the damage done with our final breaths?

How do we teach our young not to prejudge? How can we continue to pass on to each successive generation the lessons that are not only outdated but just wrong?

Why does one of us not care enough about another of us? When will we get it?

All questions. No answers.

The Shame of It All

Every place on the face of this earth where
black people exist is a place of lack.

Lack of
Concern,
Care,
Freedom,
Love,
Happiness,
Light,
Inclusiveness,
Options,
Cohesiveness,
Recognition,
Power,
Comfort,
Opportunity,
Dreams,
Hope,
Trust,
Laughter,
Peace.
Lack of everything except want and need.

What if ...?

What if certain figures in American history had been really bad at what they did or smarter about what they didn't do?

What if Nathan Hale had been a coward and refused to fight in the American Revolution?

He wasn't. He was the first black man to die in that war.

What if Paul Revere had overslept and never took that ride to announce that the British were coming? He didn't. He made the ride that eventually led to the country we live in today.

What if George Washington had been a liar and a slave owner? He was both!

What if Abraham Lincoln had been a liar and a slave owner? He wasn't, and he became the builder of the American dream.

What if Frederick Douglass had been ignorant and illiterate? He wasn't.

What if Harriet Tubman had a poor sense of direction and led the slaves back to the South? She didn't.

What if Martin Luther King, Jr. had been lazy and refused to march and risk his life? He wasn't, he didn't, and he paid the ultimate price.

What if Emmett Till had stayed home in Chicago that summer? He would have lived.

What if OJ had not divorced his first wife? He'd still be rich, famous, and revered instead of reviled.

What if Barack Obama had not run for president? He did, and if not, we would not have a health care system for the Republicans to tear apart in order to doom the poor.

What if our current president were sane? He isn't, and we must be vigilant and an advocate for each other as they are out to get us as they make America great again.

What if we woke up tomorrow in America and all was well and equal and fair? We won't. But if we don't educate and enrich our children and those less fortunate we will continue to suffer the consequences. We won't even be able to remember a time not better than the present. We have allowed the electorate to screw us all. We didn't go to sleep at the switch. They snuck in when we were looking. We held the door open for them. The citizens obviously did not look behind the curtain. Not even when the facts were right there in their faces. The only saving grace will be when the system has finished screwing us all those of us who knew better and tried to do better will survive. Because we've been screwed before—it's a familiar theme here in the United States of America.

What if there was an inexcusable display of hate in Charlottesville, Virginia, leading to the death of a human being? There was, and the president failed to stand up for the citizens of this country and speak out clearly against hate. He is a disappointment to nearly everyone except his base. Long live ignorance. It is the one thing that the USA has a never-ending supply.

What if ... You fill in the blank.

The New Genocide

Some years back, there began a new trend. The killing of minority men, women, and children. At first, there was outrage among the minorities. How could the killing of unarmed men, women, and children be justified? Well, we soon learned just how. The brave police, men and women of this nation, could simply say "I feared for my life" or "I thought he was reaching for a gun" when there was actually a wallet or phone in the hand of the soon-to-be deceased.

How do we reconcile this? Aren't the police trained to be better than this? Why are there no whites being killed for these ridiculous reasons? They run away. They use and buy drugs. They are more likely to be armed than a minority simply because there are more of them and they readily observe their Second Amendment rights. Do minority men and women have the right to bear arms? I guess not.

The egregious handling of these cases is more outrageous than the cases themselves. This is the new genocide. No hiding necessary. No faking of the evidence. No real reasons offered. It's the new genocide. No hood required.

Reflections on the Day

At the end of the day, when it's all said and done, ask yourself the following:

Did I do harm?
Did I shame?
Did I humiliate?
Would my parents be proud?
Have I held to my values?
What would my children think?
Am I guilty of selfishness?
Can I stand in God's presence without fear?
Did I enhance?
Did I do anything good and right?
Did I make it better or make it worse?
What more could I have done?
What can I do now?
Did I stand for those who could not stand for themselves?
Can I make it good, can I right the wrong?
When I lay my head down, will the sleep of the innocent come to me, or will I suffer the fate of the wicked and sleep no more?
Tell those whom you love that you love them.
Take nothing for granted and leave no stone unturned or kind word unsaid,
Because at the end of the day, when it's all said and done,
All you can do is your absolute best,
As we, the master race, the human race, move forward.

Hostile Environment

From the beginning, we have lived and worked and tried to play in what can only be called a hostile environment. Imagine if everything you did, every act you committed, every thought had and everything you tried to accomplish was deemed inferior. Every breath, every move, everything worthless, with few notable exceptions this is the black American experience. Even now. Accomplishments are slowly acknowledged if at all. We now know that we would not have made it to the moon without the brilliance of black women who worked at NASA but were given no credit until decades later. Why could their accomplishments not be recognized? What harm would have come from the recognition? I fear this will become the norm again if we are not vigilant and verbal in our observance of the new norm. We must not rest and take anything for granted. We can too easily lose the little ground we have gained over these many years if we are not attentive. The environment is even more hostile now. Minorities are undervalued and dispensable. We come from shitholes and the country must be walled off to keep the undesirables out. Imagine where we could be as a race, the human race, if all that hate and energy could have been used to further our causes instead of widening our divide. This is the final frontier. Nothing else in this life is certain. We need to value each other for our humanity, not hate each other for our differences.

What if our children grew up completely color-blind, never having to have known the pain of the previous centuries? Wouldn't that be something?

Freedoms

This country, founded upon the foundation of freedom, has become a country of few desirable freedoms. The citizen who works hard and raises a family has little protection under the law. The constitution guarantees life, liberty, and the pursuit of happiness. This is a fallacy that applies only to the majority because that is for whom the document was written. You work hard to educate yourself, get a good job, and raise a family and buy a home. You sign a mortgage and pay off student loans. You obey laws and send your children to college. Then what? As retirement nears, your property is devalued and the institutions you trusted walk away with everything you owned. What is your recourse? You have almost no recourse. A few years back, they took our homes and our pensions and the futures of our children. Then what? They were deemed too big to fail, and the government rescued them with the tax dollars we paid. What did we get? Literally nothing, the chance to start all over again at an advanced age. But again, we trusted, and what did we get this time? Now we are faced with the chance to be killed in a nuclear war caused by two men who have reduced the fate of the world to childish name calling. More of us will be uninsured, unsafe, overly taxed, unable to buy a home or educate ourselves, and ill-prepared for the future while leaving our children ever more debt. The America we live in stands for the few not the many. The haves and not the have-nots. Very few freedoms. When will us plain folk get a chance? I say never. When will our turn come? Exactly one day after never. So what we have is the freedom to hope and dream, work hard and fail, plan well and be cheated, to raise our children to look forward to a dismal future all while having no expectation that more than a few fortunate ones will make it.

So continue to work hard and raise your children well. They are our revenge, for they are the only hope for the future. Our reward most probably will not come in this life. Keep faith with the one true source of all freedoms. He's never made a promise He didn't keep.

What would Jesus do?

What kind of a system of justice forces a person to plead guilty by coercion and intimidation? This is a rhetorical question because of course the answer is "Ours does." The innocent can be arrested and indicted on the word of a single person motivated by any kind of nonsense. The alternative to not taking a plea is so devastating that admitting guilt to something one did not do seems the lesser of two evils. With so many variables and possibilities for a miscarriage of justice, the system is poised to swallow up the poor, the undereducated, the minorities of the world. The reality is that you can't win without a good lawyer and God working in your favor. The system is so skewed against the poor and minorities that it requires serious fixing.

The system is simply broken. We continue to pretend to love liberty while we ruin the lives of citizens who deserve so much better but are caught in the web of fake justice. The United States of America is the biggest fallacy of all. We punish on the basis of race, gender identity, socioeconomic status, fame and fortune, political aspirations, expediency, or any other reason that strikes the fancy of the police or status-seeking public officials.

This is what we have after Jesus Christ came to show us all how it's supposed to be done.

The Health Care Debacle

Here in the greatest and most progressive nation on earth exists an idea that the poor and the homeless and the unfortunate have only themselves to blame for their collective lots in life. These are the undesirables who have limited use and are disposable. Every child born has the inherit right to every good break out there. We forget that the billionaires and industries who rule this country have a very different idea about it. Health care is an inherit right. It has nothing to do with socioeconomic status. We suffer from all manner of illnesses, some congenital, some genetically passed, some acquired by circumstances, some by choice. Some caused by stupidity and greed. No matter. All people deserve the right to have good and competent healthcare at a reasonable price. Caring for a sick loved one should not destroy a family's budget. Deciding whether to buy essential medicine or have food to eat is not a choice that should ever be made in a country such as this. Something is very wrong.

We have allowed certain industries to exist and knowingly endanger its employees. When the inevitable happens, no one takes responsibility. The resulting illnesses are denied. Black lung and mesothelioma are two examples that feed the legal system twenty-four hours per day. We have allowed the military to harbor criminals within their ranks who prey upon the weaker male or female only to close ranks and deny that military sexual trauma is a major issue affecting male and female personnel. The general public would be shocked to know how many people, male and female, are harassed, assaulted, and raped while serving in the military only to be shunned and disbelieved when it is reported, if it is reported. You know that there are no privates out there raping generals. These acts are committed by ranking members on lesser ranked members. And by those of equal yoke committed upon each other. Add to that the combat-related tragedies. PTSD is real.

All these situations and so many others too numerous to name have one thing in common. They can only be solved by comprehensive and integrated health care carried out by competent caregivers. Other so called lesser nations have been able to solve the problem of health care delivery. Why can't we do the same? We have the best of the best right here, don't we? We solve the problems of the universe, but we can't figure out how to solve the problem of caring for our own people regardless of race, creed, color, age, or any status. Caring for the sick or infirm is one of the criteria upon which we are judged as a nation. If we allow suffering to prolong itself because of a question of dollars and cents, we must take our place among those unevolved and uncivilized nations run by dictators and idiots.

When President Obama took upon his administration the task to deal with health care, he knew the fight he had started. Good people joined him and put their careers on the line to give us all the chance for good and affordable healthcare. Many lost those careers. Others lost the ideal that this is a great country. The insurers and pharmaceutical companies seized the opportunity to stuff their already bulging pockets with more cash while cheating the public out of what the spirit of the health care fight was all about.

What good are medicines that are unaffordable? Why do the research and testing only to price the end result beyond the grasp of those who need it most? What is the endgame? Who benefits except Big Pharma? Insurance is useless if the deductibles and copays are astronomical.

The health care question is one that demands a response sooner rather than later. The right has had eight years to come up with an alternative to the Affordable Care Act. They have produced nothing reasonable. They continue to put party over country by not participating in a bipartisan solution to an overwhelmingly important issue. As we wait people are suffering and even dying. The aged, the young, the unborn, the working parent, the susceptible, the weak, the teens and tweens, the healthy and the public at large all require health care even if it's only preventative, which is the most important kind of all.

The Place We Now Occupy

This president has forever diminished our standing on the world stage. We're are no longer the best … the greatest … the land of opportunity. Not anymore. We are a small and petty and greedy and selfish nation run by small and petty and greedy and selfish billionaires who are uninformed and who don't know the meaning of grace or gratitude. This president and his cabinet and his minions and his family have reduced the USA to microscopic insignificance.

It will be difficult to get used to not being the arbiter of the world and adjusting to our present status of being has-beens. We stand for nothing because those who voted for him fell for his con game. He showed you time and time and time again what a snake he was, and still you blindly fell for his empty senseless lines and chants. He has made Bernie Madoff look small-time. They have swindled us out of our country, a country that was not so great anyway. We fully have our problems with race and wealth and equality and hope and fairness and pride and evil and such. But we have never sank so low as a country as we have now.

As a nation, we are mean and stupid and vindictive and hopelessly lost. We can't help ourselves let alone anyone else. History will bear out that this is one of the darkest periods of our time … When we sat idly by and buried our heads and turned a blind eye to what has happened. We have given our nation over to fools and children who dreamed of playing war games and dress up and doctor in the White House.

A bunch of old white men and a couple of old women who are as despicable as they come. Yes, they have bullied their way into positions of great authority, but they can't pull it off.

A Reason to Kneel

In the state of Georgia, there were 171 cases of the police shooting and killing civilians from 2010 to 2015 according to the *Atlanta Journal-Constitution* published on October 11, 2015. Needless to say, the majority of these victims were minority men and women. To date, not one case has ever even gone to trial. How can this be you might ask? The judicial system found a way in each case to continually and conveniently close the cases without the perpetrator, the cop, ever being tried for these horrific killings, usually by manipulating the grand jury system. All over the United States, minorities are killed, most without reason or provocation, only to have their slayings hushed or covered up by the authorities who serve and protect.

According to the article, Georgia has a unique approach to allowing the police to kill citizens and get away with it. I think they are wrong. I believe every state in the union is more than prepared to allow the wholesale killing of minorities by law enforcement. People are choked to death, shot, staged suicides, phones and wallets mistaken for weapons, left to seize while cuffed in the back of a police vehicle, female officers confronted by big scary men, children walking with sodas and Skittles in their hands and folks selling cigarettes or CDs/DVDs on the street. All very legitimate reasons to shoot someone in the head or beat them to death if they happen to be a small female.

It is almost impossible to hold your hands up while getting your driver's license out unless of course you have three hands. Every state has numerous and shameful stories to tell about how the public has been treated. Thankfully, most of these stories don't end in death but an alarming amount end fatally. There are real criminals out there who must be dealt with in a violent manner at times in order to keep safe those who serve and protect. The problem is that so many of these cases are so easily pushed aside that the police almost have carte blanche and little fear of the same legal system of which they are part.

In this country, a white female whose sensibilities are bruised when spied on through a mirror nets $55 million in a settlement. Though having been violated, she is still alive and able to work and live and laugh and love. These dead minority men and women are gone forever and some pathetic amount of cash, if any at all, is offered in exchange for a life wrongly taken. When we consider the number of lives forever lost to poor policing, we can only conclude that law enforcement in the USA is still in its infancy having not evolved so much.

This is why Colin Kaepernick took a knee.

Party Over Country

As 2017 comes to a close, we can say that we have witnessed some of the most unbelievable and outrageous events of all time starting with the current presidency whose repercussions will be suffered for decades to come. In an attempt to delegitimize the previous administration, he has set the course of history back for even more decades to come.

It isn't just that he is unaware and unconcerned of what is good and right. He has collected a group of, like himself, insanely rich, unfeeling, limited-minded people who are out of touch with reality as most of us know it. They are automatons who put party over country no matter the results. He has chosen a staff of sycophants who feed his ego and run at his beck and call for fear they'll be the next to hear, "You're fired." Most of these people are serving outside of their areas of expertise, whatever that might be.

The lies and covering required to make this administration appear to be functioning is astounding. I'm sure someone somewhere is calculating the number of boldface lies and misrepresentations told by this administration. The total will be Guinness Book worthy.

Their chosen candidate for Alabama senator harkened about how slavery was a better time in this country. Any non-white who voted for him should be shot (figuratively) to protect the species. The mind cannot absorb how these people continue to live and thrive in modern days.

After the election of this bigoted man who sexually harassed/abused women, made fun of the physically challenged, was too stupid to recognize cultivation when he was experiencing it, and dodged the draft five times, it is not hard to imagine that he would declare war on the legitimate media. He has done this not realizing how this might further damage our world standing and our ability to stay informed of the truth.

We await the day when all is revealed on the issue of Russia when it is finally shown just how backward thinking this administration and the Republican Congress has been. None of these people have any credibility. The Republican Party has chosen to support and follow a man whom the majority of them cannot stomach. Rolling back the accomplishments of the previous administration and replacing them with hurtful, shortsighted, and greedy measures. By the time his base finally wakes up, they will be scratching their heads and their butts wondering what happened. No health insurance, no coal mine jobs, rampant racism, and an extra trillion in debt. He has made America great again—a great big laughingstock that may never recover her standing in the world. How you like him now?

Making America Great Again

We live in a country that, to those who know no better, represents freedom and opportunity. Rights and lawfulness. Good rather than evil, a place borne of struggle and hard work by people who wanted a different experience and who fought to make it a reality. A place where all would be welcome to start over. That's what made America great.

Almost immediately, the tides changed. The land they believed was uninhabited was sprawling with natives for whom they had not planned. America, you have a problem. Next was the need for laborers because after all, they were land owners and pretend barons; they could not be expected to work the land that they now know is stolen. They decided to kill the natives and join the slave trade to gain laborers rather than use their wives and sons and daughters or to actually pay people to work the land. No. They desired free labor. These two events began what made America even greater.

The slaughter of one race and the enslavement of another. Things went on like this for a very long time as these settlers became more powerful and greedy. There was little resistance or difference of opinion to what became the status quo for centuries. To this day, the struggle for equality and recognition continues.

Now fast forward to 2016. This is the year a perfectly qualified female candidate would be manipulated out of the presidency in favor of a man who mirrored the early settlers. A man who is greedy, power-hungry, an unintelligent poser who though he showed the world the kind of man he is, was still elected, with or without the help of the Russians. Some believe that is still yet to be determined. In a few short months, he has shown himself to be incapable of the office. He has ushered in a return to the good old days. His principal goal is to undo/undermine/delegitimize the Barack Obama presidency. It is that simple and that obvious. Because of his lack of a skill set and the people with whom he has surrounded himself, he can't get a thing accomplished except by executive order. He cannot govern. He cannot negotiate successfully. He has failed on a massive scale delivering on almost none of the promises he was elected to put through. The sycophants who have shamed themselves by working for this modern-day tyrant will never again have credibility. This man is narcissistic, and his ego must be fed regularly. They make sure he dines well. Through his crew and the work they do for him, he has signaled a return to coldhearted policies aimed at the least of all Americans. Children, the elderly, minorities, women, and the poor have no chance under his rule of law. The few victories that we had are being scaled back at an alarming rate.

So if you think this is the place to be, stop and think again. It's no better here than in some third world countries for some of us. Many will not welcome you or value you. In an atmosphere of hate and lack of sensitivity, America has become a family dynasty characterized by doublespeak and destined for ruin and civil war again. We will not stand for our rights and privileges to be taken. They have been too hard fought and won and much too shortly enjoyed. Whosoever is pulling the strings has done a good job. They have played the long game expertly. So well, we never saw it coming. But they have underestimated the real people in this country. Sadly, we may all end up paying the highest price of all because they have made America great again.

An Appeal to the President's Base and All Others Foolish Enough to Have Voted for Him

Now comes this man who would be president. Known best for reality TV, he makes the mistake of winning the presidency. He was more shocked than Hillary. You've put a man in the oval office who brags about committing sexual assault. He started a war with the media and believes he can prevail. He has embroiled himself in a web of deceit and lies. I understand that you wanted change, but you completely disregarded reason in your search. When a man shows you who he is, accept it.

You were all so single-minded in your cause. You had to cleanse yourself of the presence of the previous president, so you voted for change, and change you got. You got chaos and incompetence and daily drama as well as crime and mystery and best of all you got Russia. The one consistent element about the president is his cover and protection of all things Russia.

You have a White House spinning from the uncertainty of the day. Who'll be fired or demeaned or shamed into submission? What revelation will come to further shame this country? Who will he offend next? How will he further embarrass this country? The cast of characters is never dull but often disappointing. How low can we go?

There's an attorney general who got caught lying when he answered a question he wasn't asked. There are serial liars and cheaters who abuse the privileges of their jobs. The sad thing is that they do know what they are doing. They want to return to a way of life long gone but not forgotten.

We are all equal by virtue of our birth. No man can change that because it is our God-given right. No man can determine another's destiny by force or hate. It may appear so in the short term but not really. Good will prevail; we just don't know how damaged our society will be by the time the president and Russia get done with us.

It's sad because you thought you were trading up. You put your money on a mule, and you thought he'd be a triple-crown winner. You blinded yourself to what was glaring you right in the face. The problem is you are bringing us all down with you. We didn't buy a ticket for this horrendous ride, but we can't get off. Every passing day diminishes us before the world. Take heart, we'll prevail, and we will eventually forgive you.

Media Mania

Let's talk about the media. There is no question that a free media is indispensable in a democracy. To attack the media is to attack the right to question, investigate, expose, exonerate, and apologize, to name a few. The free media is what stands between the populace and the madness that would be allowed to rule without it.

Recently, social media has been named as a culprit in an attempt to destroy our way of life. As Americans, it is our duty to think for ourselves and our children and those who cannot think for some reason. It is our duty to ferret out the truth. Simply reading something or hearing it on television is not good enough. We must reason and ask ourselves who, what, where, why and how. We must figure out if the info we are being fed is inaccurate or truthful, if the sources are reliable, if we can count on its conclusions, and if we can govern ourselves according to those conclusions.

Fake news has become more fashionable than ever. The president refers to anything that he doesn't agree as fake news. Because he is a fake president this is not a surprising revelation. The citizens of this country must be ever-vigilant to the tricks and outright lies that masquerade as news. We must expose ourselves to multiple sources of news and ideas. We must be well-rounded to be intelligent enough to think for ourselves.

The fact that a foreign adversary was able to infect our election is frightening, to say the least. The fact that a large section of the populace doesn't believe it happened is horrific. We play into the hands of our adversaries when we appear weak and divided. Unless we want to wake up some morning singing the Russian national anthem, we must get our collective acts together and fight this latest attack on democracy, lest we forget this is a worldwide attack.

So the next time you hear something odd or read something strange that is labeled as news, take the extra step to educate yourself before passing it on as factual. Remember, anybody can put anything on the internet and dress it up as the gospel. People can report anything in print or on television and call it news. Know your sources and trust your instincts. Be your own source. You should be able to trust you.

The End Is Near

As I sit here in the cold dark of the morning, I try to recall a better, happier time. It is difficult to remember such a time. Recent events have cast a negative shadow on all Americans. Those who do not realize it are far worse off than those who do. We are in a time where the world truly hates America and thereby Americans. The media has been called into question. Stop and think … Where would we be without the free media? Under the rule of our current president, we have come to a place of senselessness. The white house is so full of negative characters set on destroying this country and recreating it in their own image that it is as a runaway train, fueled by hate, fear, and money and destined for total annihilation. Think that sounds extreme? Think about it in real time. Before the election in 2016, we were on a productive track. Whether or not you supported President Obama's agenda and that of the most recent ex-presidents, there was not a feeling that the country was under the control of someone else. Like a ventriloquist dummy, we are being played for stupid. We are distracted by so much crap that it requires real attention to keep up with all the slick tricks the real power structure is handing out. It is an extension of the supplying of drugs and the proliferation of the prison system. It is not about elephants and donkeys; it's about race superiority. Hitler's clones are alive and well and masquerading in many forms. Race cleansing is happening, genocide is happening, and the wall is already up, right here in the good old USA. Carried out by those in power—the real power. Not the politicians or the police, but the people who control the politicians and the police. Those who sit back and quietly run this country. Through the use of blackmail, money, sex, and other pressures exerted on the weak who have stumbled into "power," we all have a part in this psychodrama, whether willing or unwilling.

This book has been an attempt to shine a very bright light on the serious problems we as a nation must face, some humorous and some not. It has also been a reality check for me. I feel as though I live in a country under mob rule, as though those trusted to run this country are flawed beyond all hope, as are we the public. Our thinking has been reshaped and warped because we're too lazy to pay attention and stay informed. The very problem of police misconduct, racism, and brutality is what started me on this tract. As time and life revealed, our problems are complex and compounded, and I was driven to speak of many of the devastating issues we have created for ourselves. The gist is this: we must stop the systemic and pervasive abuse, mistreatment, and degradation of minorities in this country. As always, we look to the good folks in the majority to aid us in this fight. This is how it has always been. Change comes when those who have the real power finally realize their responsibility to the world and the future.

Our children must be allowed to be born into a world of true equality and opportunity. The road to true equality and opportunity is a minefield littered with the bodies of the innocent. This has come to be seen as the norm and therein lay the problem. It will never be acceptable to kill or mistreat the poor, the homeless, the mentally ill, the targeted minority, or the disenfranchised, to name a few. We gotta do better.

The End

"So dark, the con of man."
—*The Da Vinci Code*

This is how plain commonsense folks think. This is what happens when we watch the news and scream at the screen, wishing we could offer some common sense in the moment. What Colin Kaepernick started was a movement. He chose to stand for something by kneeling for something. He is to be congratulated. He is one of the few who actually did something that brought all kinds of hurt upon him and his family, and I know he wouldn't change it for the world. Those who live in fear of the masses tried to turn his message into a side show. Aided by the president, they were almost successful. We all have to find the strength to act, to be uncomfortable, to find a way to make this world a better world. Forget all you hear about going to live on another planet. We will all be dead long before that is a reality. We have to live here, on this planet, together. With each other and for each other.

I call for a complete overhaul of the legal system starting with how we choose our police officers. The screening process must be fine-tuned to exclude the racist, violent, or heartless officer. To protect and serve is an honor. It should not be seeded to those who are unworthy simply because their forefathers served or some political favor has been called in. We must start with the police academy and extend change to the Supreme Court, hitting every rung of the ladder in between. We are not all suited to this calling and some of us are more of a danger to society when given the keys to the jail and the legal system. Minorities go to prison for the same infractions that whites are granted probation. This cannot continue.

Let me say that it will never be acceptable to kill or mistreat the poor, the innocent, the disenfranchised, the mentally ill, or the homeless. How did we arrive at this point? This country touts itself as the best of everything there is to offer. This too is a fallacy. Some of the most divisive, small-thinking, ignorant people on the planet have participated in the creation and ruination of this country. I'm talking about from its inception up to this very day. Greatness defines itself. It requires no advertisement. It is immediately recognizable. Everybody knows greatness when in its presence. What we have here is not greatness. We have failed on multiple levels. We, collectively, are the human race. While I am sure there is more intelligent life out there until they show themselves we are stuck with each other. We are all we have. So we better get on with the business of respecting and loving each other or we are all doomed. Not just the undesirables—but all of humanity as we know it.

These very fallible human beings are now the architects of the dismantling of the bedrock of this country, the most important branch of law enforcement of the USA. The reason for this is simple: they have chosen to protect the president and the Republican Party at all costs. This is historic and shaming. What these people have forgotten is though they wield the power now, they will not always. The balance will shift as it always has. They have not considered what the long-term repercussions will be. There is a redeemer. We will have to give an account of our actions, and we must not forget these times when we enter the voting booth. The current party of the majority has acted with reckless disregard for anything except the politics of the moment. They have not given a thought to history or the future. It is absolutely obvious that the president has been and may still be involved in the destruction of our democracy.

Greatness is defined by how we treat the least of us—the weak, the poor, the sick, the aged, and our children and the other species upon which we depend for survival. By this measuring stick, the USA has been a 242-year failure.

"So dark the con of man."

About the Author

Bradley Long was born and raised in the Midwest during the 1950s. His idyllic childhood ended when his brother was thrust into the middle of desegregation in the sixties achieved by the integration of schools and was bussed to what had been an all-white school. Life was never again the same. Since that time, he has been acutely aware and tuned in to race relations in this country and around the world. The more recent rash of slayings of minority men and women in this country by law enforcement served as the impetus for this book. This is one person's take on how far askew we as a nation have gone on the subject of equality and how we must to get back to basic principles of understanding, tolerance, and hope.

www.ingramcontent.com/pod-product-compliance
Lightning Source LLC
Chambersburg PA
CBHW031417250726
48656CB00002B/709